ALPHABREATHS

Sounds True
Boulder, CO 80306

Text © 2019 Christopher Willard and Daniel Rechtschaffen

Illustrations © 2019 Holly Clifton-Brown

Published 2019

Book design by Ranée Kahler

Printed in South Korea

Library of Congress Cataloging-in-Publication Data

Names: Willard, Christopher, author. | Rechtschaffen, Daniel J., author. |
  Clifton-Brown, Holly, illustrator.
Title: Alphabreaths : the ABCs of mindful breathing / by Christopher Willard
  and Daniel Rechtschaffen ; Illustrated by Holly Clifton-Brown.
Description: Boulder, CO : Sounds True, 2019. | Audience: Age 4-8.
Identifiers: LCCN 2018040903 (print) | LCCN 2018044453 (ebook) |
  ISBN 9781683642800 (ebook) | ISBN 9781683641971 (hardcover)
Subjects: LCSH: Respiration--Juvenile literature.
Classification: LCC QP121 (ebook) | LCC QP121 .W55 2019 (print) |
  DDC 612.2--dc23
LC record available at https://lccn.loc.gov/2018040903

10 9 8 7 6 5 4 3 2 1

ALPHABREATHS

THE ABCs of MINDFUL BREATHING

Written by
CHRISTOPHER WILLARD
& DANIEL RECHTSCHAFFEN

Illustrated by
HOLLY CLIFTON-BROWN

sounds true
BOULDER, COLORADO

A

Alligator Breath

Open your arms wide like alligator jaws on the in-breath. Snap them shut on the out-breath.

B Butterfly Breath

Spread your arms like beautiful butterfly wings on the in-breath, and let them flap gently on the out breath.

Cake Breath

Breathe in as you imagine a birthday cake. Breathe out as you imagine blowing out the candles.

Dolphin Breath

Breathe in as you lift your arms up high. Breathe out as you imagine diving into the ocean.

Elevator Breath

As you breathe in, imagine your breath going all the way up to the top floor of your belly. As you breathe out, imagine it going all the way down to the bottom. You can even count floors as you breathe.

Flower Breath

Breathe in and imagine you are smelling your favorite flower. Breathe out and imagine you are blowing the seeds of a dandelion.

Gratitude Breath

As you breathe in, think of a person you're grateful for. As you breathe out, send them a smile.

Hugging Breath

Close your eyes, give yourself a hug,
and gently breathe in and out.

Ice Breath

Sit very still like you are frozen in ice. Notice how your body moves as you breathe in and out.

Join Your Breath

Join the rhythm of your in-breath and out-breath with a friend, so that you are breathing in and out together.

K

Know Your Breath

As you slowly breathe in and out, check in with your five senses. What can you feel, hear, taste, smell, or see?

Lion Breath

Breathe in, feeling brave and strong like a lion. Breathe out, letting out a powerful (but quiet) roar!

Mountain Breath

Breathe in and breathe out while keeping your body still like a mountain.

Ninja Breath

Pretend that you are a ninja. Breathe in and out as silently and slowly as you can.

Oatmeal Breath

Breathe in and imagine you are smelling a bowl of hot oatmeal. Then breathe out like you are blowing on your oatmeal to cool it off.

P

Perfume Breath

As you breathe in and out, what perfume can you smell in the air?

Question Breath

As you breathe in, ask yourself how you are feeling. As you breathe out, answer.

Redwood Breath

Breathe in and reach your arms up high like branches extending to the sky. Breathe out and imagine you have roots growing from your feet deep into the earth.

Superhero Breath

Breathe in and imagine you are a superhero. Breathe out and imagine how you will help someone.

Teddy Bear Breath

Lay down on your back and put a teddy bear on your tummy. As you breathe in and out, watch your teddy bear go up and down.

U

Underwater Breath

Paddle your arms, imagining you are underwater. Breathe in and out, blowing bubbles through your scuba gear.

V Voice Breath

Take a big breath in and sing
Laaa as you breathe out.

Wish Breath

Breathe in and make a happy wish for yourself. Then breathe out and send a happy wish to someone else.

X

Xylophone Breath

Imagine playing a xylophone from the bottom to the top on the in-breath. Then play it from the top to the bottom on the out-breath.

Yawning Breath

Breathe in a big, mindful yawn, paying attention to all the sensations you feel. Then let your breath out.

Zzzz Breath

Imagine falling asleep. Close your eyes, take a big breath in, and hold it. Then slowly let out your breath, imagining a long *Zzzz*.

To Leo and Mae
— CW

To all the kids who invented these breaths as we
taught, learned, and played mindfulness together
— DR

To Sasha, Shiloh, Inka, Honey, and Oshi
— HCB

ABCDEFGH
KLMNOPQ
STUVWXYZ
ABCDEFGH
KLMNOPQR
TUVWXYZ

ABCDEFGH
JKLMNOPQ
STUVWXYZ
ABCDEFGH
JKLMNOPQ
STUVWXYZ